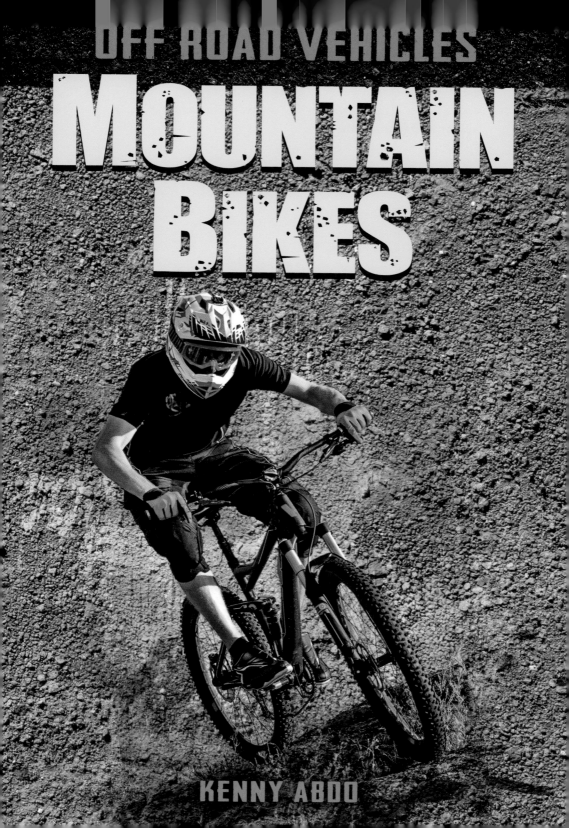

OFF ROAD VEHICLES
MOUNTAIN BIKES

KENNY ABDO

abdopublishing.com

Published by Abdo Zoom, a division of ABDO, PO Box 398166, Minneapolis, Minnesota 55439. Copyright © 2018 by Abdo Consulting Group, Inc. International copyrights reserved in all countries. No part of this book may be reproduced in any form without written permission from the publisher. Bolt!™ is a trademark and logo of Abdo Zoom.

Printed in the United States of America, North Mankato, Minnesota.
092017
012018

THIS BOOK CONTAINS RECYCLED MATERIALS

Photo Credits: Alamy, Getty Images, iStock, Shutterstock
Production Contributors: Kenny Abdo, Jennie Forsberg, Grace Hansen
Design Contributors: Dorothy Toth, Neil Klinepier

Publisher's Cataloging-in-Publication Data

Names: Abdo, Kenny, author.
Title: Mountain bikes / by Kenny Abdo.
Description: Minneapolis, Minnesota: Abdo Zoom, 2018. | Series: Off road vehicles |
      Includes online resource and index.
Identifiers: LCCN 2017939282 | ISBN 9781532121043 (lib.bdg.) |
      ISBN 9781532122163 (ebook) | ISBN 9781532122729 (Read-to-Me ebook)
Subjects: LCSH: Mountain Bike--Juvenile literature. | Bicycles--Juvenile literature. |
      Extreme Sports—Juvenile literature.
Classification: DDC 796.63--dc23
LC record available at https://lccn.loc.gov/2017939282

TABLE OF CONTENTS

MOUNTAIN BIKES

A mountain bike is a bicycle meant for **off-road** cycling.

Some of the first mountain bikes were made in 1896. **Buffalo Soldiers** fixed bicycles to ride from Montana to Yellowstone National Park in Wyoming.

Today's mountain biking began in Northern California in the 1970s. Bikers would ride older, single-speed bicycles on mountain trails.

TYPES

Mountain bikes have three main designs. Hardtail bikes have some suspension.

Full-**suspension** bikes make for a comfortable ride. But they are heavier. Rigid bikes have no suspension.

Mountain bikes also have wide, knobby tires. These help bikes move on many types of **surfaces**, like dirt and gravel.

Mountain biking is broken down into many categories. Some are cross country, downhill, and trail riding.

The US held the first national Mountain Bike **Championships** in 1983. The first **UCI** Mountain Bike World Championships were held in 1990.

Mountain biking joined the Summer Olympics at the 1996 Atlanta Games. Dutch rider Bart Jen Brentjens won the gold!

GLOSSARY

Buffalo Soldiers – members of an all-black military unit who are well-known for their service in the Civil War.

championship – a game, match, or race held to find a first-place winner.

off-road – riding a vehicle on difficult roads or tracks, like sand, mud, or gravel.

Olympics – the biggest sporting event in the world that is divided into summer and winter games.

surface – the top layer of something.

suspension – a system of springs and shock absorbers by which a vehicle is cushioned from road conditions.

trail – a path created to travel through rough terrain.

UCI – short for Union Cycliste Internationale, the world governing body for sports cycling and international competitive cycling events.

ONLINE RESOURCES

Booklinks
NONFICTION NETWORK
FREE! ONLINE NONFICTION RESOURCES

To learn more about mountain bikes, please visit abdobooklinks.com. These links are routinely monitored and updated to provide the most current information available.

INDEX